That's Why
I Love You, Mama!

A Story of Love That Only a Child Could Tell

Aaron & Maria Hoffman
Illustrated by Jerry Werner

LOYAL KIDS

SISTERS, OREGON

There's a light still on downstairs

when I go to bed

You're still working hard

so that I might be fed

I want to thank you MAMA.
You do your best

In my eyes you're better than all the rest

That's Why

I love you Mama

You build me up

when others seek to tear me down

When I blow with the wind

you plant me on solid ground

Greater Love

has no one for me

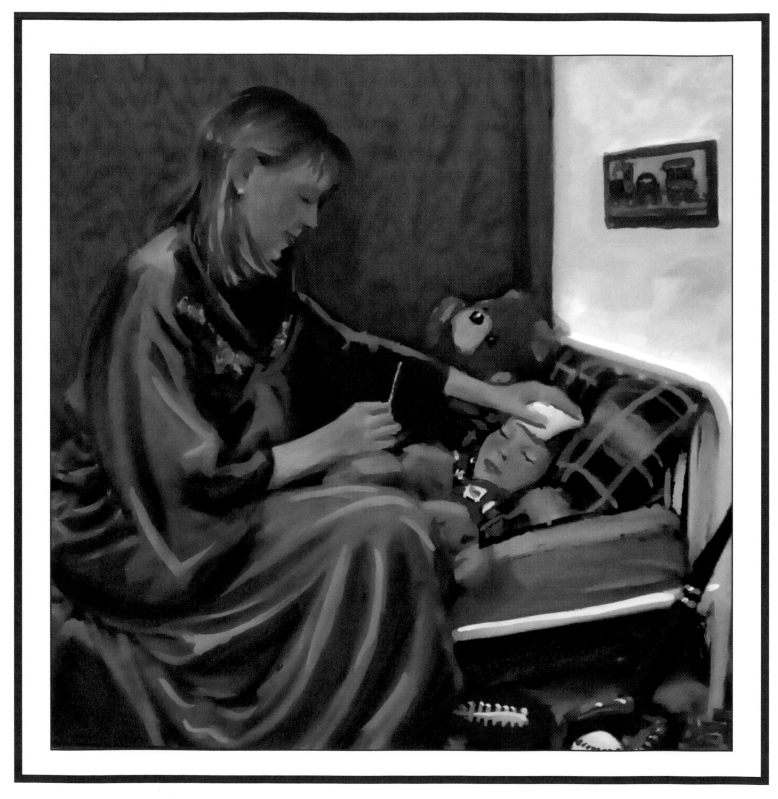

You would give your life

a thousand times for me

That's why

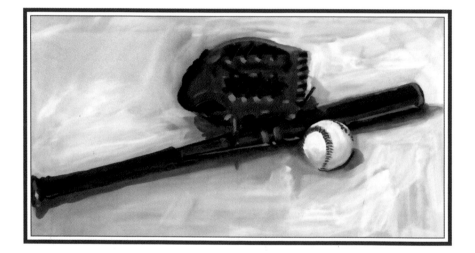

I love you, Mama

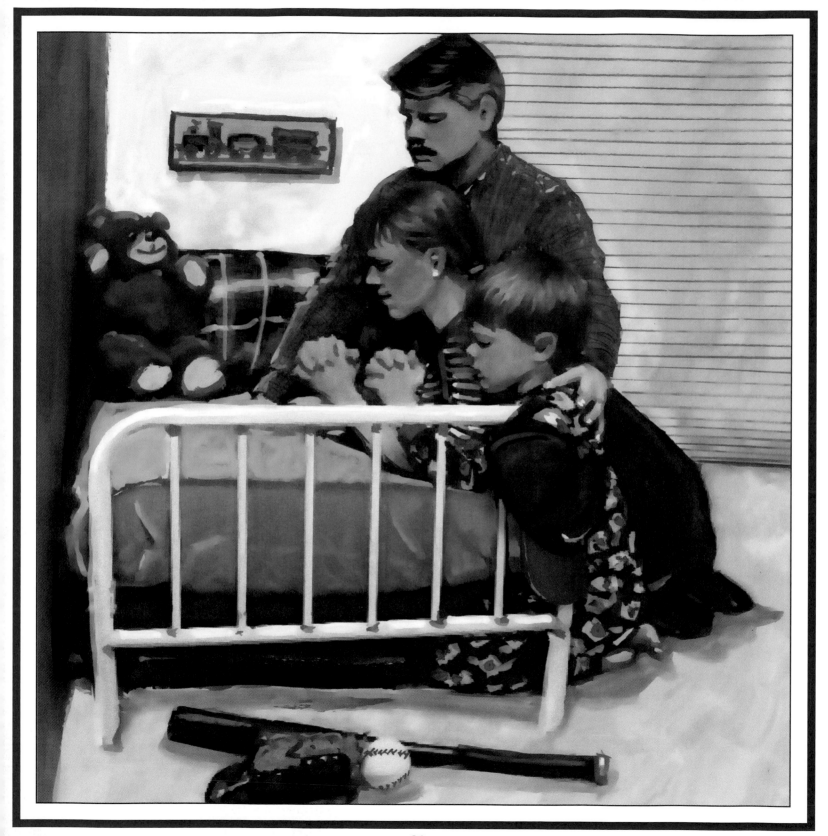

I love the way you pray for me

beside my bed at night

And press me on

to keep in the fight

I didn't do a thing

to deserve your love

Such a perfect gift

That's Why

I Love You, Mama.

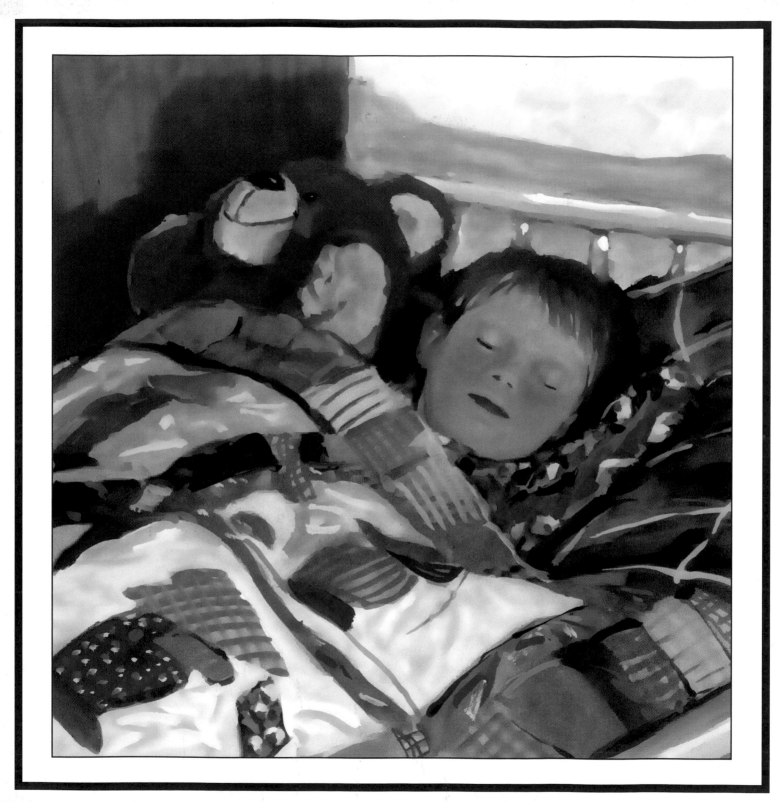

There's a light still on downstairs
when I go to bed.

That's Why I Love You, Mama!

A Story of Love That Only a Child Could Tell

Published by Loyal Kids

A Division of Loyal Publishing, Inc.

P.O. Box 1892, Sisters, OR 97759

www.loyalpublishing.com